Over Ea

Poems by
Chris Searle

with drawings by
Martin Gollan

To Cliff and Paul,
Enjoy it like
we have!

Chris
9/11/2021

I am going to fight capitalism even if it kills me.

—Sylvia Pankhurst

Forsooth, brethren, fellowship is heaven and lack of fellowship is hell;
fellowship is life and lack of fellowship is death; and the deeds that ye do upon
the earth, it is for fellowship's sake that ye do them.

—William Morris

First published 2021 by **Culture Matters**.
Culture Matters promotes a socialist and progressive approach to art, culture and politics. See www.culturematters.org.uk

Text copyright © Chris Searle
Drawings copyright © Martin Gollan
Edited by Mike Quille
Layout and typesetting by Alan Morrison
ISBN: 978-1-912710-42-3

Foreword

By Chris Searle

These poems were written between January and April 2021, during lockdown. I wrote them as I looked out of my window over Eagle Pond in Snaresbrook, East London.

The path along the pond's northern edge is a favourite place for pram-pushers, dog-walkers, duck-feeders, small children with their parents, joggers, lovers and pedestrians, and the road beside it is a direct route to Whipps Cross Hospital. On the other side of the pond are the grounds of Snaresbrook Crown Court, built as an orphanage in 1843.

Sitting in my flat during these lockdown winter mornings, watching everything outside being projected on what seemed to be a technicolour screen, it was as if poems came tumbling out of me in a way they had never done before. I began to think of poets, artists, activists and revolutionaries who had lived close to the pond and who may have come here in times past.

They included Sylvia Pankhurst who lived a couple of miles north during the 1930s in Woodford, where she organised her endless campaigns for working women, against war and the Italian fascist invasion of Ethiopia; the rustic, bird-loving poet John Clare, held in an asylum a few miles away, and who escaped confinement in 1841 while the Snaresbrook orphanage was being constructed; the artist, poet and pioneer revolutionary socialist William Morris was born just east of the pond in Walthamstow in 1834; the film-maker Alfred Hitchcock, born over his father's grocer's shop in Leytonstone High Road in 1899—did he devise the narrative and screenscape of his film *The Birds* from remembered boyhood visits to the pond? All these humans from the past, and many more from the present, visited and provoked my imagination as I looked through the smudge and condensation on my window, all through those cold months of lockdown dawns.

The poems are dedicated to all those brave and brilliant people who work and struggle within the National Health Service.

I'd also like to thank Mike Quille of Culture Matters for his supportive, committed and skilful editing work, and for introducing me to the powerful artistry of Martin Gollan, whose empathetic and inventive drawings have added vividness, humour and depth to my own very ordinary words.

Contents

Early Morning Across The Pond

the white shadows
 of phantom swans are smudged
 through the wet panes
 of falling water windows
 dripping with the condensation
 of the long damp night
subdued squawking is suppressed
 as the dayclean rises
 with the growing hum of cars
 and the gothic lines of the
                courthouse turrets
 and fallen tree trunks on the
                far pondside
 hide the virus from our fears
the morning is slow arriving
marked by a dawdling milk float
and early joggers, never deterred

if you catch the moments
 through the melting darkness
the dawn comes like daily promise
 provoked by humans, even here
 at this time, in this era
 foreday morning in the heart of hope

Little Red Bus

every twenty minutes
along Snaresbrook Road
comes the little red bus,
    W12 is on its front
    with passengers of courage
    NHS humans socially distanced
    inside their masks
staring from the windows
eyes over the pond
    as the gulls swirl
    as the coots dive
their images of freedom
before donning PPE
before mopping the wards
before pushing the trolleys
before making a hundred beds
before proning their patients
before telephoning their families
before risking all
    heroes and humans all
sitting on a bus to Whipps Cross Hospital
rolling past the pond
    early in the morning
    late in the evening
    heroes and humans all
    ordinary people like us
    on a bus to Whipps Cross

Iced-Up

the gulls stand on the pond
it is another way of knowing water
the banks are stiff with frost
and the coots slip and slide
searching for an ice-hole
in a quest of life
    halfway across the pond
    a jagged line marks an end to ice
    it's like a frontier
    and the swans have colonised
    the water beyond
    and they swim freely
    as the ducks try to make it theirs
ice has magnified divisions on the pond
increased the arrogance of species
while humans pass in their masks
and pull their dogs on leads

Carnival of Covid

they step, they run, they amble
carefully, singly, in couples
in families, in bubbles
this is a strange carnival
on a winter Sunday
all along the pondside
between and below the fluttering gulls

their mouths are shut away under cloth
their nerves lively
        their blood warm
in company and friendship
        and solitude too
they are a procession of the willing
of all who want it all to pass
but a weekend walk along the pond
will be a small breath of freedom
to sense the birds doing
        what they cannot do
to let their minds and dreams
        fly over East London
to settle on the trees' high branches
and hope with folded wings

we say it all the time to the world
stay safe, dear humans
it will not always be like this
as Bertolt once wrote
long is not forever
        as the ducks quack on

Coots

busy they are
always busy
   diving, disappearing
then their black heads surface
   shaking at the joggers
   or the children on scooters
they seem to come up close
and eavesdrop on the ducks
swim warily near the swans
and take no notice of
   the swooping gulls
they are activists in feathers
imperturbable ever
what do humans matter as they pass
with their worries
with their stringent masks
they bob and they dive
   always urgent
   always finding something
   sticking from their beaks
pearls of Snaresbrook plenty
in this shallow pond

Ada and Joe

their car slowed to a careful halt
over double yellow lines
next to the path by the pond
yet no law stopped them
and they do this every day

Joe got out of the roadside door
    watching for traffic, left and right
he walked around the bonnet
to open Ada's pavement-side door
grasping her and pulling a little
smiling under her white hair and a peaked cap
as she emerged in a cloud of gulls
and Canada geese squawking

her wrinkles smiling
she held his arm as they walked
    their daily walk
just fifty yards or so up the pondside
and back again to the car
who knows the words
    they had for each other
but every aged movement
    is one of love
years of love still blooming
    as the leaves fall over the other shore
and float on the pond
    between the gabbling ducks

he helps her back into the car
then walks around the bonnet again
waiting for an ambulance to pass
    then a white van and deliveroo bike
back behind the wheel
he turns around in an opposite drive
in a semi-circle of daily devotion
before they drive off
until tomorrow
    same time, same place

Pond Sunset

a haunting purple covers the sky
and a far plane trails a line of smoke
   across the cirrus clouds
over the trees on the pond's far side
the shades of red hang like curtains
as four swans rise and flap
   the full width of their muscled wings
   power them over the trees
just a few moments of the day's farewell

I see on the screen of my windows
   a technicolour film
   scarlet on the water
rippling the reflection of the sky

if you look hard
the shallow turns deep
while the far seems close

close of day
   open the darkness
the world and its virus
   ever mutating
as its birds caw and babble

Swans

sometimes they act
like white supremacists, frost-white
as if this small pond
were their Mississippi
and their birthright were
   to assert their ownership
   their white dominion
as they menace the mallards
as they chase the coots
   their necks like pikes
   their beaks like blades

other times their love shines
   a family love
   their browning cygnets
   always close to them
   ever protecting them
   white and warm
   with feathered flesh throbbing
   teaching them to fly
   as they rise in glory
   their wings of beauty
      soaring for freedom
      while human eyes marvel
all along the breadcrumbed pavement

Fox

fox hobbling
fox with an injured leg
crippled he is
yet it doesn't stop him
climbing on the garage roof
  looking at men and women
  in the darkness
  coping with covid
his fourth leg won't touch the ground
it hurts too much
  yet his eyes gleam
  red balls in the darkness
staring at the humans

does he know
what the humans have
as they jog along the pondside
as their children throw bread to the ducks
as they push their prams of hope
as they stride to catch the tube
  at Snaresbrook Station

oh fox, in this world and out of it
with problems of your own
with your three-legged walk
searching for food
  among the closed-up bins
how could you know how the humans feel
how could they know
  your hidden fears
covered by your rain-soaked fur
  all in this world

Sirens

how they whine
   they whine
   like animals with wheels
   they whine

with brave humans inside their cabs
   they whine
they go to find covid
to find strickened hearts
to find strickened brains
   they hurry, they speed
   they whine

where would we be without them
   and their blessed whine
as they hurtle past the pond
as they scatter the ducks and gulls
with their caring, loving whine
so deep inside our ears
so deep inside our blood
whine of rescue
   whine of hope
   whine for us all

Teacher

he stood, holding his bike with one hand
and binoculars in the other

I came up three yards from him
    are you an ornithologist, I asked,
my mask vibrating with the words

well, I'm a birdwatcher, he said through his
    I often come here

I know, I've seen you before
    through my window, I said
waving at my flat
    I live up there

his beard pulsated as he spoke
    about the black-headed gulls
    the diving ducks
the young swans, their feathers still tan
as their parents flapped their wings
and took off with a daily majesty
for the pond's far end

he told me about the aggression of the coots
as a black mother threw bread towards them
and her child clapped her hands in glee from her pram

however he called himself, he loved the birds
he educated me about them, me
an old geezer in a mask
standing on the pond's edge
    I loved his lesson

Visitor

I woke yesterday morning
through the window's condensation
   to see a sable swan
   just one, alone, visiting
her contrast with her white mates
    blinded the wavelets as they rippled

she swam to the pond's western edge
under a wooden notice with Morris' words
telling us he was born in this borough
and reminding the earnest joggers
the masked pram-pushers
   fellowship is life

she swam in ebony glory
through the black-headed gulls
and skittering coots, all in company
her head held high on her stretching neck
proud, solitary, defiant she looked

today gone elsewhere
   remembered in wonder
   an instant is a lifetime
   through a misted pane of glass

Canada Geese

that's what they call them
   Canada geese
once I emigrated
I lived there for four years
I never met them there
but now
   here in London
I see them every day
   hear them too
they swim and they walk fearlessly
   along the pondside
   looking for human gifts
   bread and seeds
they walk with the people
unafraid and equal
are they from Toronto
are they from Alberta
   Winnipeg or Yukon
did their forebears fly
   from Nova Scotia's shoreline
   or the Great Lakes
   or the pine forests of Ontario
to find this East London pond

nowhere could be less like
   the Canada I once knew
   Lake Moraine in the Rockies
   the prairies of Saskatchewan
   the steelworks of Hamilton
but here they are, supping London crumbs

along the Snaresbrook kerbside
telling me one more time
we live in one world

Poem To Thoreau

I look over the pond
   it's not like Walden Pond
   it was made by humans
   in the company of nature
once a gravel pit
it drank from a brook
they dammed it up and made a pond

Thoreau saw heaven in his pond
he built a cabin by it
he wrote his book and
   its transcendental message
   went out to the world
and he drank its Massachusetts waters

I don't see heaven here
but I see the birds and humans
and a love for the dark earth
   the sun-glistened water
the water is shallow
I could walk through it
   to the other side
yet its spirit provokes mine
here, deep in London's cosmopolis
in a time of plague and fear
the soaring wings above it
the human steps beside it
the bird limbs below it
   swimming invisibly
fill me with life and hope

Shadows On The Pond

the gulls make white dots on the shadows
cast on the wavelets of the pond
menacing shadows
the skeletons of leafless winter trees

swans swimming
   cut furrows across the water
   like floating ploughshares
   on this dark covid afternoon
   as coots dive and disappear
   as a woman jogs by with a white headband
   and a man strides by, holding two leads
   one with a boxer, the other with a greyhound
   and a Sikh with a blue turban
   and a half-opened umbrella

they're all moving reflections
of Snaresbrook's flickering mirror
   of a local, worrisome world

Prisoners In The Vans

where do they come from
those in these long white vans
with dark oblong windows
with Serco on the chassis
where do they come from

is it Pentonville or Holloway
is it Wandsworth or Brixton
or is it Belmarsh
    the cruellest they say there is
or Yarl's Wood
    the 'immigrant removal centre'
removal and sexual abuse
a last place to know in England
before they fly away
    and not like these birds

electronically tagged
    and enclosed they are
in a cell with wheels
which passes by the pond
and scatters the gulls
and the green-necked ducks
with shining feathers
as they turn in the courthouse entrance

who knows Serco
and their 500 contracts worldwide
I, said Edward Argar, government minister
    and Serco lobbyist

I, said Rupert Soames, chief executive
    and Churchill's grandson
I know Serco from Iraq to Sydney
    from Mount Eden Prison, New Zealand
    to asylum camps in Christmas Island
I know Serco and those who look for refuge
I know Serco and its frauds
    and its deaths in custody
    and its culture of self-harm
I know Serco and its prison vans
as the winter sun streams on the pond
as the joggers dodge their splashes
and the bemused babies in prams stare
I know Serco
I know the £108,000,000 in their pockets
for the failures of test and trace
    outsourcing lives!
    outsourcing lives!
and the prisoners in the vans
sit cramped in their compartments
    as the swans of Eagle Pond
    take flight above them

Poem For Michael Rosen

you said after 48 days
   in intensive care
and you were writing again
   that 'the page remembers'
it does Michael, it does,
it remembers well
it remembers that Covid is a Nazi
that it kills in its millions
and only unity will save us
   like it did before
that no human is an island
that the NHS is our mainland
all the humans on the bus to Whipps Cross
cleaners

      porters

        nurses

          doctors

            clerks

all the people who work and serve
those who work for us
        between us
          with us
all the prepositions of life and love
that we learned at school
that we use in our poems
that we write and speak to the world
in the countless languages of the ordinary
that we use in London
that walk and talk beside this pond
and carry their meaning inside these words

for five months I tried to follow
    your agony
    your progress
    your healing
I spoke with you today
your words through the wires
every one was still as strong
as laced with humour
as bloodstreamed with humanity
you're here, you're with us
and every learning child
    that reads and hears your words
every teacher who shares your urgency
    here

        now

            today
shining as the blinding sun
    glints on this pond
    and breaks through
    my misted windows

Islands

at the far end of the pond
there are two small islands
they are the nesting places
their raised earth
   is covered by
   duckshit, swanshit, cootshit
but no humans go there
among the shrubs and stunted trees
it is birdland
and only their lullabies sound there
under Morris' three human words

and I remember Donne's words too
and what they meant to Mike Rosen
as his lungs pumped in and out
   the precious frantic air

no swan is an island
no coot is an island
no gull is an island
no duck is an island
and every wilful jogger knows
as she passes. as he passes
puffing out that same London air
no human is an island, even like these

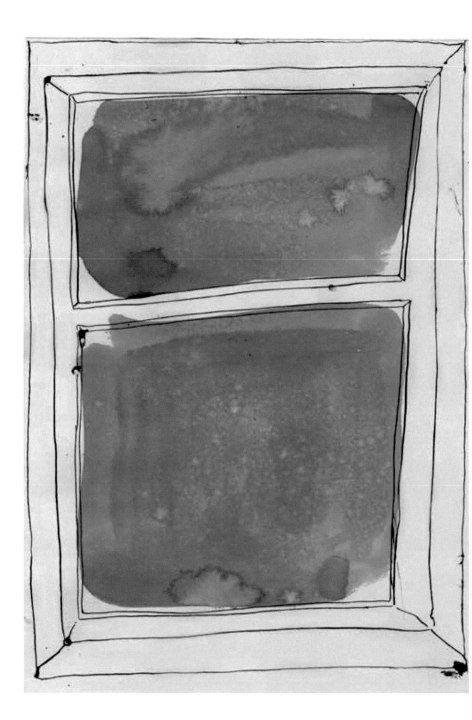

Wiping

every morning around five o'clock
I wipe my windows
the glass is covered by dripping water
it makes a swamp of vision
as I look through, the world is wetlands
there is no Grasmere Vale
   no Tintern Abbey
   no country churchyard
   no pleasure dome
the pond becomes a marsh
the courthouse seems spectral
its one lighted window
   a mottled star
the first jogger has a light on his cap
its beam shines on the kerbstones

my cloth is sodden with
   the window's night moisture
but now I can see
the morning's first bus
and a man in a mask
stares from its glass
and as my glass clears
   I can see a local world
   and all the excellence of the ordinary
and its humans start to thrive again

Joggers

joggers of the cosmos run here
for this is London
they cruise along the pavement
   they sprint
   they canter
   they power-walk
sometimes they hustle to finish before work
other times they are slow as slow can be
they wear T-shirts of American universities
or canned drinks
   or slogans of love
they are from Somalia and Slovakia
   Brazil and Bahrein
   Trinidad and Finland
   Melbourne and Bangkok
   Hong Kong and Vancouver
but now they are here
   now
   running
facing the virus with fitness
dodging the prams with
   finesse or clumsiness
   all Londoners now
all in motion in a far-flung city
at home as the gulls soar and plummet
as the ducks quack for bread
as the scooters overtake them

truly
   running for their lives

they are mostly young and lithe
but some have white hair
   pressed under their caps
   with legs like sticks
   and bellies round and full
it is as if running defines them
nothing will stop them now

Buggy Riders

she's always in front
steering between the joggers
around the dog-leads
carefully dodging the prams
Sandra's the pilot
   she carves out a path
   and Dennis keeps behind
his eyes are fixed on her wheels
his specs are perched on his nose
I feel like Stirling Moss on this thing
   he tells me bashfully
or maybe even Lewis Hamilton

how long have they been together
their movement is electric now
but did they once walk lovingly
through Leyton Flats and the Hollow Ponds
   their arms interlocked
   her hand in his
   his arm around her waist
   their flesh joined as one

they're on separate saddles now
single-file and distanced
they come back from shopping
with Tesco bags of food
   it's an expedition done
   an excursion fulfilled
they'll find their legs and feet again
in the late Snaresbrook morning

7.15 a.m.: Getting My Paper

I like the cool air in the mornings
　　and beholding the swans
but I don't like the walk
having to side-step fellow walkers
with yards between us
　　crossing the road to avoid
　　a couple abreast on a narrow pavement
it's not the way to live
　　not the way to find union
　　not the way to find fellowship
　　not the way to be a person

I pick up a *Metro*
rub sanitiser on my hands
　　in Snaresbrook station lobby
adjust my mask and cross the bridge
my *Morning Star* is waiting
　　at the newsagent
the Asian shopowner and I
　　have our daily greetings
　　and a few friendly words
　　be safe, be careful, he says
　　you too mate, I say
and I'm walking home
when a black-bearded locksmith comes stumbling from his shop
waving a wiry broom at a scuttling mouse
who runs into a gutter
　　as the darkness comes to light
as it always will
whether we're here or not

Courthouse

on the far side of the pond, it rises
its twin-domed towers
   give it a neo-Gothic semblance
   and its powerful windows
   in their stone frames
   stare straight into mine

the gulls in their scores
   rest on a fallen tree trunk
   poking into the pond
they stand like sentinels
   the black rectangles on their heads
   picked out from their white feathers
   are like the caps of hanging judges
   perched from my boyhood

once an orphanage
then a school
now a courthouse
   this is a protean building indeed
and the Serco vans circle its history
holding its subjects, all enclosed
do they look from the windows and see the birds
   no eagles now
do they see the freedom in their flight
   the power in their wings
   the community in their flocks
   the love in their coupling
wheeled cells of Snaresbrook
   cells of covid
and the sun glints like fire on the pond

Mrs Ali's Blues

with her grey grey locks
and her black bag
   of brown bread, wheat and barley
leaning hard on her stick
with her eighty years
she staggers to the pond every morning
   sharp on eight o'clock

all the ducks know her
they are there waiting
every morning by the kerb of the pond
and they celebrate her coming
with an avian joy, a dawn festival
   today she has a special bag
   plastic, sealed and see-through
when I pass it looks like popcorn
she empties it into the water
and the cinema of nature opens its screen

Hitchcock grew up a mile or so away
over his Dad's grocer's shop
did he ever see birds like these
did they always peck into his memory
when he sat in his Hollywood director's chair
a boyhood walk from Leytonstone
to the flock and gaggle of Eagle Pond
and women with bread like Mrs Ali

she told me
    I come here every morning
    when I get up
    I get a lot of pain
    it's the rheumatoid arthritis
    but I've got to keep moving
    keep moving all the time

she smiles and walks off
    her stick is tapping
    her bones are bending
    the birds are eating

Poem For William Morris

I wake up in a rage, William
   angry at our rulers, our controllers
not so different from those
   who outraged you
those who let the virus jeopardise us
those who welcomed it at our airports
those who refused to prepare
         refused to test
who shovelled the infected elders
         out of the hospitals
and sent them back to care homes
in all their aged innocence
         infecting thousands more
killing a generation they told us
         to respect and love
those who gave test and trace
         to their cronies
who outsourced it to multinationals
         who lock us up
whose mobile cells pass your words every day
         'Fellowship is life'
those who are the contrary
         of your words of love

do you remember how you roused the people
   at Dod Street, I do William
do you remember the unwavering words
   you spoke to thousands
   when they buried Alfred Linnell
   that day in Bow

Fellowship is Life

do you remember the ordinary people's
   beauty you created
   in every loving fabric
   every pattern of living
   every word of inspiration

now this threesome of words
   proclaimed on a notice board
   next to our pond
   fill me with an obstinate hope
   as the gulls wheel over our heads
   and the sun makes fire
   on the water

Remember Captain Tom

across the pond
the waterside trees are close together
and I think of Captain Tom
   he died today

when he was a young man
he walked with his mates through jungles
squeezed by the sodden trees
forgotten armies of young brave men
heroes and freedom-lovers all
in the year I was born

they were crushed and smothered
   in the Burma swamps
drowned in their rivers
shot down along bush paths
enslaved in the prison camps
building railways and struggling with malaria
while Europe found its peace

forget all those who trade
   on fame and celebrity
   on his brave life and death
remember the old men like Captain Tom
walking up and down his garden drive
a long, long way from Burma
for another country, the NHS
a hundred times for a hundred years
in pain too, like his Burma comrades
making 32 million kisses of care
for unforgotten armies of now-times heroes
telling us and showing us countless times
that tomorrow will be a good day

Nighat's Gift

masked up, I walk past the pond
sanitising my hands
   as I pass Morris' words
I'm going for my vaccination

I step apace to Wood Street Station
I wait at the barrier as a young official
   tells me through her mask
   trains are delayed
   there are animals on the line
animals in Walthamstow?
what creatures are these?

half an hour we wait
good job I was early
when the driverless train arrives
just two stations and I am there

I can't thank the driver
out of the station
   and up St James Street
to Franklin's pharmacy on the main road
a short wait and I'm in the booth
a young woman, Nighat
   makes me feel like family
she checks my particulars
she laughs through her mask
she reminds me of the girls
   I used to teach
I don't feel her needle

two days ago this place was a shop
today it gives us vaccine
   long live the NHS
   long live Nighat
   and all who work with it
we owe you our lives, our futures

I walk back to the station
   trains are regular
   the animals are gone
I'm back home quickly
   and as I pass them
   I look up again
   at Morris' three words
never have they been so true
and a cup of tea
never felt so good
my arm is painless
yet filled full of hope

Two Little Boys

two little boys pass with their mum
bobble hats they're wearing
and riding blue scooters

as they pass
   a swan rises
   chasing some audacious gulls
   boldly blocking its route through the water
its wings flap on the water's surface
making swishes, a percussion of fear
these wings are bigger
   than the boys' bodies
they ascend from the pond
   with a violent grace
stopping the boys' rolling wheels
as they stare, transfixed

how it brings back my own boyhood
watching swans and ducks
   in Raphael Park, Romford
tossing out bread
learning how to count
by counting ducks and moorhens
beginnings and endings of life
   by urban ponds, shallow and grey

77 Years

the first sirens I ever heard
   were not like these
they were the sirens of the doodlebugs
sunk deep in my memory
77 years ago it was
   the Blitz they called it
   East London had it bad
   as my Dad put out the fires
   and dug up the buried and the bombed
   the sirens were never-ending
   and the Russians stood staunch in Stalingrad
   and plans were made for D-Day

now, epochs later, in my last grasp of life
I sit here at my window, watching the walkers
wondering what they're wondering
as the gulls swoop over the water
and the ducks squabble for stale bread

hearing these new sirens
   as the ambulances hurtle past
I the watcher, watch on
   and listen today
the first day of my 77th year

These Old Words

every new morning
I feel like a projectionist
I pull back the red curtains
   I see shadows on the pond
   and as the darkness gradually ebbs
it is pandemicolour
   with sky
        water
            trees and earth meeting
and the birds waking
   chuntering to a new covid morning
   and the first joggers and vans
   pass by the camera of my eyes
and the screen of my imagination

and if you breathe the moments
and if you commune with the birds
and if you see the humans
   through these old eyes
   these old words recycled
   every morning's beauty comes alive

even now, even here, with these birds flying
and can their wings take us
to the afflicted in Manaus
to those excluded in Gaza and Ramallah
to the townships of the Cape
to the frontierlands of the Rohinghya
   birds, birds take us there
   even in our minds
   from this small pond in Snaresbrook

Dazzle

sun dazzling on the pond
     makes me blink
makes more water come to my eyes
     as I try
to look direct from my window
a jagged line of shimmering sun
broken only by a bent metal post
     with a cycle symbol
     knocked awry by a fast car
     at an acute angle now
bringing the brilliant sun to reality
even the tripping dogs' eyes moisten
as the heavens flare on the pond
in the midst of winter
and the sun comes to Snaresbrook
unknowingly bright

Were You Here, Sylvia?

every day I wonder
did Sylvia come here?
up the Woodford Road
she lived in a cottage
        a red cottage
where she wrote ceaseless letters
battering those in power with her words
about their love of war
their profits from war
their hatred of justice
their contempt of working women
for the ordinary
    men and women
who now too
    walk along the watershore
and stare across this pond
holding their phone-cameras
like third eyes to catch a sunset
or the glorious uplift of rising swans
    were you here Sylvia
did you think about your next letter to power
as Mussolini's fascists invaded Ethiopia
as the Nazis built their death camps
as Jews and Roma were murdered in millions
    in the land of Beethoven
were you here Sylvia
thinking of your next sentence
    in your head already
    the next letter
as the swans swam towards you

ONLY THIS AGE
THAT LOUDLY BOASTS
REFORM HATH SET
ITS SEAL OF
VENGEANCE
'GAINST THE
MIND

FELLOWSHIP
IS
LIFE

did you bring them bread Sylvia

I stood over your bones once
    under the eucalyptus trees of Addis Ababa
but were you here Sylvia

Duck

Oh duck, duck
    ordinary duck
    working duck
I think of where I've lived
    where working people
    called me duck
where bus drivers told me
    thanks duck
when I passed them the fare
where supermarket women at the tills
called me duck as I filled
    my plastic bags

duck, as you swim and dive
    ordinary duck
    brown-feathered duck
    common duck
    open-beaked duck
    everyday duck
    duck of my heart
duck so human, like me

Abi And Ollie As The Sun Goes Down

it's still winter
but Abi and Ollie sit by the pond
    they're holding hands
    their legs are over the pondside
    shoes close to the water
they're whispering
looking closely at each other

what are they saying
as the sky turns red above them
what cue does it give them
    what blood-words does it provoke
    for they are alone now
    alone only for seconds
    as the gulls whirl above them
before a skinny greyhound sniffs them
and its owner pulls it back

what young dreams are here
in the midst of the pandemic
in the hearts of lovers too

The Mist Rises

the mist rises
    from the still, still pond
    like smogs of boyhood
mist like lies
    which whiten the truth
the lies about PPE
the lies about care homes
the lies about test and trace
the cronyism of death
the profiteers of people's misery

the mist rises like an accounting
the jetstream over
    the lucid orange sunrise
points at the truth like hope

Mid Morning

the Etonian nightmare of Johnson's face
    dissolves in the water
    calmer than calm
its only lines the darting swims of swans
and the surfacing of the diving coots

a young father lets his son
    loose from his papoose
he staggers along the pavement
    too close to the pond's edge
his Dad picks him up with a flourish
    the boy has a tantrum
he sits him on the pavement
    he is screaming
    his legs are flapping
    his lungs are bursting
but the gulls don't hear him
as they soar over the water
it is mid morning over the pond
but what is time to them

What's In A Pond

what's in a pond
    its waters are shallow
    its boundaries are small
    dammed-up one end
    tiny islands at the other
unspectacular, mundane
path and road one side
trees and courthouse on the other

yet the coots find plenty
in their five-second dives
ducks peck floating bread crumbs
the grey water holding food
the shores giving nests
    waterlogged tree trunks
    fallen homes for gulls
swans breeding families
    proud cygnets trailing their parents
    learning new adulthood
    testing their burgeoning wings

and humans too with their children
    all along the pondside
a mother and her son
is he five or six
stop by the sloping 'cycles' sign
he pushes, pushes, pushes
tries to push it straight and upright
unmuscled but eager
with all his boyhood strength

it's not enough
he kicks the sign
and walks away head down
his mother following, calming
what's in a pond

I Look In The Pond

this morning
    walking by the water
    as the spectral mist rises
    I look in the pond
    below the still shallows

I see a phantasmagoria
I see the ghouls of now-times
the moguls of untruth
crooks in the littered water

I see Johnson
    Trump
    Netanyahu
    Bolsonaro
    Modi
the butchers of Myanmar
grinning below the surface
with their local racketeers
    Gove
    Patel
    Hancock
while honest humans pass
on their way to honest work
to feed and clothe and shelter
    the ones they cherish
    in this worst of times
    which births the best of humans
    yet below this surface
    the fiends still grimace
    and rule our world

Incomers

pecking pigeons
    strangers here
this is not Trafalgar Square
no pigeon ownership here
not proprietors here

    what's in their minds
    when they see the teeming gulls
    the swans' mighty uplift
    the squads of quacking ducks
    the busy humans jogging past

here on the breadcrumbed pavement
the pigeons scour the cracks
searching for what is left
    this is not their realm
    they have the nervous look of interlopers
    of vassals
no wonder they're rare

the others shun them
look askance at them
Snaresbrook strangers
in the midst of a thousand wings

Riposte To Myself

what am I
an old man sitting on a sofa
looking out the window
   onto concrete, trees and water
   and all the birds of Snaresbrook

   probably not much time left
   but time enough to know and see
the humans of the world
   trying to make sense
   of a savage pandemic
   which is killing some of them
   and provoking them to struggle and to win

still they walk with power and intent
and jog determinedly
and push their prams and hold their children's hands
and ride their bikes
and walk their dogs
as humans do

can I affect all this?
no, not on this sofa
but I have words
messages from behind this glass
   not much
   but words
as Buddy sang when I was a boy
with simple eloquence
   words of love
for lives of love and hope

Poem For Jeremy

It's up to us, Jeremy
    all those of us who know
    know in certainty
    the lies you live through
    it's up to us to tell the truth

they hate anyone who is honest and truthful
    like you are
these sheikhs of lies
    you called for the many not the few
    enough to rile their blood
    enough to upset their governance of power
    the power that falls into their laps
    their quest for all the ego in the world
    the dung of racism
    the vanity of dominion
    the sludge of corruption
you had none of that
yet you got as close as anyone has
from the streets of the ordinary
in my meagre lifetime
in that house of command

    swirl gulls, swirl
the birds fly endlessly over the pond
they swoop, they dive, they rise, they rest
they tell us much about ourselves
and much about the land we love
and the travesty of those who rule it

your life soars with their wings, Jeremy
over this water, this earth,
    this concrete of London
how hard you tried
how much you gave
    swirl gulls, swirl

Silver Birch

I grew up with these
    silver was rare
    but these were common
    every front garden had one
glistening in the suburbs
precious Snaresbrook silver
black pockmarks
    scar the white trunks
    like the black-patch feathers
on the heads of the gulls
nothing could be more London than you

your leafless winter limbs hang sadly
like the minds of passers-by
and their wordless sighs
almost like a pandemic tree
you watch the humans' faces
as they worry about their families
as they shiver
    about their jobs tomorrow
what lasting sorrow
    glows in their faces
what traces
    of another life behind them
what fears of years before them

children call them zebra trees
as Europeans jog past them
    Africans too and legs of Asia
for the world is here
    and its virus
all beside one pond under one tree
    hope striking through
    the red morning sky

The Fall and The Rise

fish are dying of plastic in the Great Barrier Reef
there's plastic in the icebergs off Alaska
the sharks' bellies are bursting with plastic
    in the Mozambique Channel
barracuda are slain by plastic in the toxic Caribbean
    between Grenada and Carriacou
in Lake Ontario the smelts have stopped jumping
    as plastic particles cut into their gills
plastic bags adorn the beaches
    clutched to the pebbles of the Isle of Sheppey
and schoolkids throw plastic Coke bottles
    into the Eagle Pond
while ducks peck into plastic mouthfulls
as coots surface from their dives in rippling circles
and residues of discarded Tesco bags
make choking sandwiches with tossed breadcrumbs

how much of a fallen world
    is Snaresbrook, right here
now the poisoned apple is not the temptation
not the emblem of good and evil
    our enlightenment is plastic
    it holds everything
    it contaminates our present
    it contains our future
    masters of war make millions from it
    it is killing our future with covid
even here in London E 11
    how long
    how long can we stand up

how long can we last
without falling
        falling
          falling

but these young women know
there's a fall and a rise
    four of them are here this morning
    Rose, Asma, Charlene and Leanne
    they come every Sunday a.m.
    with their squeezing pikes and grabbers
    giant tweezers like silver crabs' claws
    they scour the pond bed from the pavement
    they lean right over the water
    they spike the submerged plastic bottles
    they drag them to the surface
    they stuff them into bags
        and carry them off smiling
    these young soldiers of nature

    women of the day after tomorrow
    who look beyond covid
    who see another life,
    and ask an old man like me to join them
    here in Snaresbrook too

Poem To John Clare

hello John
    I often think of you
    as I stare from this window
they put you in an asylum not far from here
your spirit rises with the wavelets
    of this city pond
how your imagination would soar
with the brawny wings of the swans
    no little trotty wagtails here
    waddling in the water-pudge
    but diving coots a-plenty
    make circlets in the breadcrumb-sludge

did you pass this pond after you escaped
    from your lonely cell
birds and humans were one for you
no way to separate
and how the feathers spoke to you
across the species gate

oh John, they called you fool for this
they killed you with a key
but you knew well that nature's kiss
will make blind humans see

so John my friend, goodnight and thrive
let's pledge to stay alive
plague and scourge attack us now
in the dawning we will strive

alive to work and change our world
to make it true and just
to make it fit for words like yours
a life of love and trust

Who Shovelled The Gravel

who cut down the Epping oaks
    to clear the forest
who scythed the gorse between them
who pick-axed the shallow earth
who shovelled the gravel to make the pits
who dammed the brook to make the pond
who climbed the scaffolding to build the orphanage
and shouted out their words of work
who built its domed turrets up to the sky
in my mask, among the birds
I sometimes wonder this as I walk by

Duckweed of Lies

oh, there's a protective ring around our care homes
we love our elders so much
   we'll give them a bouquet of covid
we'll clap for our health workers every week
we'll bang our saucepans and scare the birds
but not an extra penny for their pockets

we've plenty of unusable P.P.E.
   our cronies are making millions from it
   we'll make the NHS the National Nepotism Service
   it's a heaven of contracts
and if we count a pair of plastic gloves
   as two separate items
we'll double their number in a trice

the ducks hear the arrant deception
   they quack in indignation
the coots dive to escape its menace
   they disappear in the duckweed
the swans take off with their brown-feathered cygnets
   to fly above the waters of untruth

oh England! what a weaponry of lies is this

Ex-Commuters

commuters all gone
who strides to the station now
besuited with the skin of profit
with *The Times* tucked under their arms
who marches along the pondside kerb
as the sun rises over Wanstead Flats
what City is their endgame now

better for brain and body to jog
put on your trainers not your brogues
and run along the pavement of dreams
no more Houndsditch, Bank or Moorgate
Leadenhall Market has lost its shares
for a few furloughed months of covid
capital has gone for the birds

Phantom Joggers

I woke up this morning sweating
I saw the siblings of Trump
    it was a pre-breakfast apparition
    jogging through the glass
    phantoms and spectres all
jogging and laughing and blustering too
    all around the pond
    they jogged and staggered
their security people were
    all around them
guns and suits galore there were

they spluttered as they ran
the lies poured out of their mouths
the untruths turned rancid
    between their lips
their sound was the music of death
the agony of falsehood
the insult to the human spirit
    and spirit of the clustering birds too
of perjury and dissembling
in a mad race of calumny

Johnson was on home ground
    he led the way
even Trump could not keep up with him
    he won the lie-fest, night and day
as the night mist cleared
and the gulls' wings woke and flew
all along the pondside

Heron Of London

standing under the trees
    prevailing through the haze
    on the pond's other side
    under the twin turrets
    in the courthouse grounds of fear
presides another true beak
and the mallards swim around her
statuesque and straight-legged
as if her centuries pass in an instant
    heron of London
    wild justice of the pond
    I call her Azdak

bird perturbations
    their soliciting for bread
    their skimmering across shallow water
    like juries' disagreements
    like befuddling barristers' words
do not disturb her

is she giving cues to the judges
is she prompting the clerks
as the Serco vans cruise past her
is she the prisoners' friend
telling them of pride and self-reliance
    and honesty too
or does she stare at the joggers
loving their human movement
as she stands still like another tree
resolute and rigid like the trunks around her

wishing she could move like that
but as she flies away
    denying us all
    singular and solitary
    her feathers shining
    like the rarest precious metal
where does she go
like all Londoners from all over the world
    looking for justice
    looking for a home

All The Gulls Are Gone

this morning, through the glass
the sky is featherless
the pond seems suddenly empty
the water is strangely smooth
their fallen tree trunk
     still lies in the water, rotting
but all the gulls are gone
hundreds of them, gone

no more swirling beaks
no more audacious, skimming dives
no more hitchcockian swarms
the sky seems wider somehow
the budding trees more vacant
even the joggers run a lonesome track
and the swans have dominion in the waters
they've colonised the fallen tree trunk

many of us migrate
to and fro we go
     so why not the gulls?
my friend Pedro from far Valparaiso
     was slung in a cell
     by Chilean fascists
tortured and isolated he was
     in a cell in Arica
British trade unionists secured his release
and over the Andes and an ocean he came
     to settle in England
my friend Mike from Barbados
     loved his cricket

when he was a schoolboy
  he would bowl at Weekes and Walcott in the nets
they smashed the ball back at him
  with their cuts and drives
my hands still sting, he told me
he came to Yorkshire to find work and fairness
  became a careers officer
and fought racism all his life
my friend Abdul from Shaibi in the Yemen
  came as a boy through Dover with his father
he scaled the gantries, stoked the foundries
  of the Sheffield steelworks
  as his children learned English
  and found the English way of hate
now Abdul organises his people
and builds new lives with them

like the gulls we all come and go
  we go and we come across the world
  and settle and return
  and stay and leave
  as humans do

oh gulls, where have you gone
  come home, come home

Just A Pond

just a pond it is
yet the world is here
    local and whole, from everywhere
the interface of nature and the masked human
as men and women jog and saunter
as infants in prams marvel at the fluffy cygnets
and the grace and brawn of their parents
as pensioners clutch each other
    and point at the skimming gulls
as lovers hold close in a time of distance
as trees reflect themselves in a double world
and edifices of power tower on the other shore
as the coots' dives make circles in the water
    and watchers throw them leaves for their nests
as the ducks catch crumbs and seeds
    like feathered cricketers
as dogs prance and amble on leads
as bikes and scooters zip past strolling humans
every act defies the pandemic
every move steps into the future
every word, every sound holds fast to union
    just a pond it is

Tears In Tesco

as I walked out one February morning
masked-up and sanitised
a hundred gulls exploded above me
and a solitary blue tit
 fragile and shaking
perched on an outlet pipe
 from the flat next door
and stared at me nervously
a pensioned bandit with a plastic bag

the pond undulated in the winter wind
and a man with a dog
 with a large gnarled stick in his mouth
jogged past—I can set my watch by him

a simple walk is not straight now
semi-circles around those you overtake
dodging in the gutters to give space
 to those who come towards you
 and somehow smiling through your mask
 is this the way to be a neighbour?

outside Tesco I wait for the lights
 to change to green before I enter
I stop by the cereal shelves
a woman has a box of Weetabix
 and is weeping
I cannot see her tears under her mask
I cannot see the shape and beauty of her mouth
 but I can hear her, feel her pain

she's middle-aged
    about fifty I should think
is she crying for her mother in a care home
for her children whom she cannot hug
for a dear friend in a covid ward
for a lonely room in a lonely house
    I don't know, only she knows
I ask her, is she OK
she nods, says yes with her eyes
I think she tries to smile
and walks slowly to the yoghurts

    I have to say, it moved me
    meeting her like that
    one of a million humans
    in my part of the city
I came back with my milk and bread
the gulls had settled on their tree trunk
the blue tit had gone
and I, another human,
scratched my beard and wrote these words

Empty Lounge

opposite the pond
    looking over the coots' ripples
is a care home
    I'm old enough to be in it
    but lucky to be out, so far

there's a long lounge with large windows
    the residents can watch the pond, like I do
    see new life of the young birds
    the cygnets and ducklings diving
    the industrious coots building their nests
the lounge was full of waving, pointing arms
    and big, wrinkled smiles
you could see them from the pavement
and joyous, aged voices pierced the glass

but now the lounge is empty
the residents are in their rooms
their carers are nervous
    forty thousand have died
as infected elders were taken from hospitals
    by a government that never cared
    and taken back to care homes
    without care, without testing
    the virus was in heaven
    its freedom was absolute

nobody laughs and sings
   now in the lounge
no tea, no custard creams or digestives
   the garibaldis are all gone
only silence now
   misty glass, scattered tables
   unseen elders, invisible helpers
   empty chairs, dispensable lives
the water of the pond seems grey and cold

Poem For Marcus Rashford

at the other end of England
a young man remembers his boyhood
   life was hard
   food was scarce
a single mother's love was precious
her mother had seen the pelicans dive in St. Kitts
   here the coots also dive relentlessly
   submerged in the quest to eat
the ducks scramble for bread
the undulant water kicks up foam
hunger is ever visible, obvious

Marcus loves children
   children who live with hunger now
   like he lived then
wealth and fame came suddenly
   with his flashing, brilliant feet
but his people never saw his back
down in Wythenshawe
they see his wilful smile
they feel his defiant heart
they know his strategic brain
   that shames government and capital

in my old imagination's eye
I see you jogging by this pond
not a Pennine pond
not a canal in Trafford
but a London pond
you bring your pride and love

from north to south
in this grim time of cursed covid
I feel your spirit in every child that passes
and every mum and dad
whose hands they hold so closely
dear Manchester boy
Snaresbrook is your stadium too

A Hundred Years Ago

fifty years ago I taught in a school in Stepney
it was next to a churchyard
there were large mounds there
   where they buried the dead
of another plague, three centuries before
   our children wrote poems over their bones
   beautiful verses of love and hope

only a century ago
   there was another pandemic
my mum and dad lived through it
but never talked about it
   not a word
in those days they blamed it on the Spanish
even though it came from America
like Trump blamed this one on the Chinese—
it's their fault, he tells his racist thugs

my dad was eleven when the plague hit Leyton
   the pond was the same, still shining
my mum was six when it scourged Clapham
   the Common was a wasteland of humans
who did they lose as the soldiers
   came home from their agony
did home mean a walk
   by this shallow pond
better than a flooded shell crater
was it strewn with birds then too
did the foxes roam along its shoreline
after the rats and larks of the trenches

oh Londoners you've known all this before
   a hundred years ago
   did you make masks
   did you socially distance
and look at the birds with envy
was it like the war itself
too bad to talk about
to peer over the parapets of memory
too many horrors to recall
did your stories stay hung
   on the barbed wire
in the dug-outs of no-man's land

oh London, city like many of the stricken world
   remember all this now
   be ready for the next time
don't let the profiteers take power
   their cronies scoop their millions
      from the people's heartache
   the liars spin their falsehoods
   the egotists govern for themselves
   the prophets of narcissism preen their monied vanity
   the racists divide our precious unity
they have no love for humans or for nature
   for health and happiness
   unless it is their own
learn from the mistakes of now-times
love your planet and each other
make your coming centuries thrive with life and love
an old geezer's wish, over this pond

Whitechapel Boys By The Pond

in those days
   before the war of the empires and the armourers
   before the plague of the rabid trenches
   at the weekends, in the summer
   as young men paddled in the pond
   and the boys fished for sticklebacks
   and put in their hands to grab newts
   and horses pulled coal carts up Snaresbrook Road
   and girls in long dresses and cotton bonnets
     chatted by the pondside
the Whitechapel boys came with their sketchbooks
they carried their paints and palettes
Bomberg even carried an easel on his shoulder
and Rosenberg lingered behind, dawdling,
   never a rampant talker
marvelling at the trees and the open sky
while Leftwich contemplated Rudolf Rocker and revolution
   translated Yiddish ballads in his head
Winsten conjured shapes with his fingers
and Gertler span tinctures in his spacious mind

what a relief it was to step on the train at Aldgate East
to ride like cave-dwellers under the poisoned earth
   past Stepney Green and Mile End
to leave those canyons of putrid streets
those sweatshops of oppression
those straits of Spitalfields alleyways
to escape the racist diatribes of the British Brothers' League
   if only for a modicum of hours
have a drink at the Eagle Inn

and laugh, talk, imagine and paint
　　in another world of air and green

here the birds were swarming and flying
swimming and launching in pride and fire
not dead and hanging on hooks
featherless and gutted in rancid butchers' shops
　　in Hessel Street or Black Lion Yard
another world of freedom for young artists and poets
a tapestry of dreams for young socialist Jews

did they nail the mezuzah to my door frame
were their paintings coloured by these skies
were their metaphors made by this universal pond

Schoolchildren Walking Past: 8.15 a.m.

this old lifelong teacher
   grey as those remembered classroom walls
is watching from his window

what's it like being young now
   teenage humans
   children of the world
   walking to school
   only some in their masks
in the pandemic's worst time

you've been told not to touch your friends
to stay fast in your bubbles
but as you walk past the pond
   and the coots dive and disappear
   and surface in their endless circles
you still do, for you know on your pulses
those three words which you pass twice daily
   fellowship is life
   fellowship is youth
   fellowship is love, is equality
what other truth can there be
   for you and your classmates
   your arms are clasping
   your hands are holding
books in bags on backs
eyes on phones
   ceaseless tongues making words
   smiles turning fast to laughter
   pushing, skipping, jostling, sidling, tripping

what is being stored for lives of the future
what scars will stripe their endless minds
   their imaginations of fire
   their dreams and plans of betterment
   and ah, the sheer voltage of their brainpower
   their uncertain futures
   their memories of these times
will they talk about them to their children
   in the years and decades that follow
   better perhaps to be a duck
   a coot, a gull, a swan, a solitary heron
   and live in and above this pond
   and swim and fly to swooping freedom

but they are young humans, youth and life are bursting
   they will be women and men
   they will struggle in minds and bodies
   they will live on London's tar and concrete
   on its smothered earth
   in its blighted air
in their hearts, in their minds, in their wills
with the future, they'll win through

Notes on the Artists

Chris Searle was born in Romford in 1944. He has been a teacher all his working life in East London, Tobago, Canada, Mozambique, Grenada, Sheffield and Manchester. His first book *The Forsaken Lover* (1972) won the Martin Luther King Award.

He has written or edited over 50 books on education, language, literature, cricket and jazz, including six collections of his own poems. For the last 25 years he has been jazz correspondent of the *Morning Star* and a member of the editorial advisory committee of the international journal *Race and Class* for 40 years.

Chris says: *'I was writing in East London, Martin was drawing some three hundred miles north in Chester-le-Street, County Durham. He has never seen Eagle Pond, yet his drawings, so full of wit, surprise and humanity, showed the astonishing power of his imagination, empathy and technique. It was as if he were right next to me, watching and drawing the world outside of my window.'*

Martin Gollan was born in Edinburgh and grew up on one of the postwar housing schemes built on the outskirts of the city. During the 1980s he studied sculpture at Edinburgh College of Art and has worked in a variety of jobs, though he has continued to apply himself to painting, drawing, cartoons for the *Morning Star* and other publications, and book illustration, including *The Folded Lie* (Culture Matters, 2019). He now lives in Co. Durham.

Martin says: *'It's been a privilege to work with Chris Searle on his latest collection of poetry and to try and achieve an appropriate visual response to the themes, everyday events and characters that feature in his poems.'*